لسان الغائب نخواجه شمس الدين محمد حافظ شیرازی رحمة الله علیه

HAFIZ
THE TONGUE OF THE HIDDEN

An attempt to transfuse into English rubáiyát
the spirit of the Persian poet,
as felt by

CLARENCE K. STREIT

With a foreword, a proem, an epilogue, a sketch
of the life of Hafiz and a note
on this adaptation.

New York : THE VIKING PRESS : *1928*

PRINTED IN THE UNITED STATES OF AMERICA
BY ABBOTT PRESS & MORTIMER-WALLING CO., INC.

Pas sans toi,
JEANNE DEFRANCE

FOREWORD

"HAFIZ is the best Musician of Words," FitzGerald once wrote to E. B. Cowell. "I am sure that what Tennyson said to you is true: that Hafiz is the most Eastern—or, he should have said, most *Persian*—of the Persians. He is the best representative of their character, whether his Saki and Wine be real or mystical. Their [other Persian poets'] Religion and Philosophy is soon seen through, and always seems to me cuckooed over like a borrowed thing, which people, once having got, don't know how to parade enough. To be sure, their Roses and Nightingales are repeated enough; but Hafiz and old Omar Khayyám ring like true Metal."

To read these lines is to regret the FitzGerald did not give us Hafiz as well as Omar. This regret is the deeper for those who realize that among the Persians themselves (and among the Eastern peoples to whom the Persians fill the rôle that their classic enemies, the Greeks, fill in the West) Hafiz is regarded as a much greater poet than Omar.

It was perhaps a desire not to encroach upon the field of his friend, Cowell, that kept FitzGerald from turning his genius to Hafiz. Cowell's translations from Hafiz, indeed, had given FitzGerald his first serious interest in Persian poetry, leading him to begin the study of Persian under his friend's direction. It was Cowell, too, who later

unearthed the manuscript of the then obscure Omar Khay-
yám and made a transcript of it for FitzGerald. The part
Hafiz played in the *rubáiyát* that followed is mentioned
by FitzGerald's biographer, Thomas Wright, who says:

"Some years previous, as we have seen, E. B. Cowell
had translated several of the Odes of Hafiz, and to these,
to the selections from Hafiz in Sir William Jones's
Grammar and to Eastwick's translation of the *Gulistan*
of Saadi, which FitzGerald had also carefully studied,
may be traced some of the ideas which he subsequently
used in his rendering of the *Rubáiyát*. From Hafiz came
the presentment of the Deity amusing himself behind the
veil by contriving the drama of life; in Hafiz, too, there
are parallels to the lines about Kaikobad and Kaikhosru,
the morning draught at the door of the tavern, the cara-
vanserai with its two portals, and the 'cypress-slender
minister of wine.' "

That the Omar that we know should have thus bor-
rowed from Hafiz is not without savour, for Hafiz, in
his turn, had not hesitated to borrow from Omar, his
predecessor by some two hundred years. But, as Fitz-
Gerald himself asked in his *Polonius*, "What is genius but
the faculty of seizing things from right and left—here a
bit of marble, there a bit of brass—and breathing life
into them?"

Many western critics before and after FitzGerald have
shared his admiration for the genius of Hafiz, and many
besides Cowell have sought, through their versions of his
poems, to make him known in the English-speaking
world. The obscurity in which he has remained would,
however, seem to allow another effort and to encourage a

method of presenting him radically different from those already tried.

He who would serve tea in Persia, serves it in the glasses to which the Persians are accustomed, but he who would serve that tea here, serves it in cups. It has seemed to me that, in like manner, he who would give us the savour of the poetry of Hafiz would do well to serve it in a form which, being already familiar to us, does not distract from the essence of the poet.

The form in which Hafiz served the verse that brought him most renown was the Persian form known as the *ghazal.* The *ghazal* is a poem of from five to fifteen stanzas in which each stanza must be a unit in itself and need have, except for rhyme, little or no relation to its fellows. Other peculiarities that make it almost always impossible to follow the *ghazal* form in English are explained in the note ending this work.

Thanks to the genius of FitzGerald, however, we do have a form for verse in which the emphasis, as in the *ghazal,* is on the stanza as a unit, and not on its connection to those that precede or follow it. But the same genius has also made *rubáiyát* a word whose meaning to many westerners is inseparably bound to the name of Omar Khayyám. *Rubáiyát,* however, is simply the plural of the Arabic word, *rubái,* which designates a special type of quatrain widely used in Moslem countries both before and since the time of Omar.

Many of the stanzas in the *ghazals* of Hafiz lend themselves easily to the English *rubái* form, to which our ears already are tuned and in which we find the peculiar flavour of Persia requisite for any presentation of Hafiz. To put

9

them into *rubáiyát* is to serve tea not in a glass but in a cup distinctly Persian.

What I have done, then, is briefly this: From the hundreds of poems that Hafiz wrote I have taken, here and there, stanzas that seemed best to give his spirit, and I have tried to express effectively in English *rubáiyát* what they meant to me. These *rubáiyát* I have sought to arrange in an order that would meet the requirements of Engilsh verse and would yet bring out the spirit of the Persian, as I felt it.

Hafiz, it will be seen, shares the general philosophy of Omar Khayyám, as Omar shares that of men who lived before him. One might argue that little of the essentially new was left for him to say by the ancient author who (himself dismissing all hope of finding anything new under the sun) wrote: "There is nothing better for a man, than that he should eat and drink and that he should delight his soul." But who will maintain that Omar is Ecclesiastes and Ecclesiastes, Omar, or that there is not room in English literature for both?

Hafiz reminds one of the Hebrew Preacher, the Greek Anacreon and the Persian Tentmaker, but his personality remains as individual as that of any of them. If that is not made clear in this adaptation, it will be once someone succeeds in transfusing into English some of that combination of profound wisdom, subtle spirit and graceful expression which has made Hafiz known to the Persians as *Lisan-ul-Ghaïb*, The Tongue of the Hidden.

C. K. S.

Mamaroneck, New York
May, 1928.

genius = the loveliness of
deriving things from R to L
here a bit of marble there
a bit of brass — & making
life run to it.

TRANSLATION —

Conversation with a Tree
Mixed media on hardboard, 1975

October

6

Wednesday

Mittwoch Mercredi Miércoles 水曜日

PROEM

O lovely vineyard where the word is wine!
O spring where purls a music none divine!
   They who make meaning marry melody
Hold all in thrall—I would their gift were mine!

The sage may free the slave, but sages know
The wise alone may harvest all they sow;
   A boundless ocean, wisdom touches all,
But they who seek its pearls must dive below.

And some who dive with splendid trophies soar,
And some bring shells that echo ocean's roar,
   And bleeding from sea spines do some return,
While some with pretty pebbles play ashore.

With pearls they say that God makes April rain,
But here on earth do raindrops pearls remain?
   So Poetry: in Heaven, perfect—here
Who seeks a finished verse will seek in vain.
         —Adapted from the Turkish of Saie.

بِسْمِ اللّٰهِ خُوَاجَهُ شَمْسُ الدِّينِ مُحَمَّدٍ حَافِظٍ شِيرَازِي رَحْمَةُ اللّٰهِ عَلَيْهِ

1

Of roses in the night, of days that plead,
Of trifles proud, of trifles great indeed,
   Of wine, of love, and of the secret, too,
Hafiz shall sing, and sing as Fate decreed.

2

To speed desire's impatient caravan,
Is this a boon Hafiz bestows on man?
   Or mockery? Is he a sage or fool?
Is this the wheat, the flour, or the bran?

3

A runner comes with tidings—should he yearn
   To know what's in them? Is that his concern?—
One only mission has the messenger:
His message to deliver, and return.

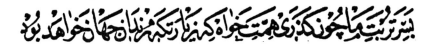

4

But stay, my son, sit here, your lips are dry,
Your news is sad, but sadder is your eye:
  What saw you on the starless trail you came?—
I saw the night unstarred in which I fly.

5

Then drink! For now the old wine-maker's heel
Stamps on night's grape! See, through the shattered peel
  A crimson juice spreads staining out! How soon
Shall parching day this wine of morning steal.

6

With childhood's Oh! we see aurora shine,
With age's Ah! we note our sun's decline:
  To go from oh to ah, from nought to naught,
We pencil but the fragment of a line.

7

We come, dismount; though swift as driven dart
We find our love, then chills the burning heart;
   The caravan bestirs, the bells proclaim
Desire already waits us to depart.

8

Yet when the Fates a moment's pleasure send,
Reject it not, but welcome it, a friend;
   Nor hesitate, for where is he who knows
How any great or petty thing shall end?

9

Within this garden sweet it is to play,
And sweeter still now that our host is May,
   No more than this can any man desire!—
But, Saki, come! Why does our wine delay?

بِسَانِ الغائبِ خَواجَه شَمسِ الدِين مُحَمَّد حافظ شِيرازِي رَحمَةُ اللَّهِ عَلَيه

10

Our stay is brief, but since we may attain
The glory that is love, do not disdain
   To hearken to the pleadings of the heart;
Beyond the mind life's secret will remain.

11

Leave then your work and kiss your dear one now,
With this rich counsel I the world endow;
   When Spring buds lure, the wind deserts his mill
And gently glides to kiss the leafy bough.

12

Examine: if your God be profligate,
For you then, too, it is a goodly trait:
   Call Saki, leave your robe of chastity—
Can you love Him and His example hate?

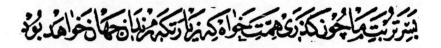

بِسَانِ الغائِبُ خواجَهُ شمسُ الدينِ مَحَّدِ حافِظِ شيرازِي رَحمةُ اللهِ عَلَيه

13

They say when Noah once regained the sod
He nursed a vine up his divining rod;
  We know when God saved him, he saved the grape:
Let us be friends then with the Friends of God.

14

Why, I once saw a monastery dean
Approach the tavern;—seeing he was seen,
  From barren temple he must turn, he said;
Where lies the grain, there must the gleaner glean.

15

When we detect in Holy Men the tone
Of truth, we can but follow: I will own
  Hafiz has never left the tavern since—
He can not leave the Friend of God alone.

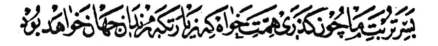

16

Seek paradise, but as you seek, beware:
Take not the border for that garden's pair;
   Ah, if at midnight you would see the sun,
Then down the veil of wine—it will be there.

17

Love hides behind the heart; despite her screen
The mirror of the eye reflects her mien;
   I, who bow not to this world or the next,
When I see love, I bow as to a queen.

18

Who fear love's fever, and who flee in dread
The throes of love—they do not know her bed;
   For me, if I may not embrace your lips,
Yet keep your foot at least upon my head.

19

Belle of Shiraz, grant me but love's demand,
And for your mole—that clinging grain of sand
   Upon a cheek of pearl—Hafiz would give
All of Boukhara, all of Samarkand!

20

As Spring draws jasmin from a barren glade,
So love draws Spring into the fairest maid;
   But you—how can I ever love enough
To give your loveliness a lovelier shade?

21

If I with Fate but once might throw the dice,
I'd try a throw, no matter what the price,
   To have my breath, O Love, be one with yours;
What need would I have then for paradise?

بِسَّانِ الْغَائِبِ خَوَاجَهُ شَمْسِ الدَّيْنِ مُحَمَّدٍ حَافِظٍ شِيرَازِي رَحْمَةُ اللَّهِ عَلَيْهِ

22

Her eyes are stars, as stars they twinkle, gay;
They tell me: Wait! wait till the end of day!
    As bright as stars her promises to me—
As bright, as many, and as far away.

23

The love within your eyes, will you declare
It love for me? I asked.   She said: I swear!
    And I knew rapture till she added: Look,
Do you not see yourself reflected there?

24

Ho, Magi! Let your conjurer once more
Dance in our bowl—we need his secret lore,
    For love seems easy, and it is a maze—
The door, magician! Conjure us a door!

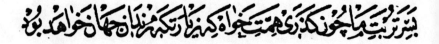

25

Indeed, the bird of love I seemed to snare;
Within my heart it nestled, unaware,
  And then the Beauty of Shiraz unloosed
Her locks: off flew the bird—and I stay there.

26

Now I, my pen, the fluid of the vine,
Together write—will He to Hell consign
  The one He made of these, my trinity?
Is he indeed Hafiz who sings of wine?

27

O wine that can transform the coward snail
Into the bounding deer! The nightingale
  Sang unto me last night; methought she cried:
My voice was made for you, O Drinker—hail!

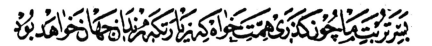

28

God keep us from these men who fatuously
Judge worth by mass, not by capacity;
    Of all the weighty things the world provides
A quart cup full has weight enough for me.

29

Friends, singers, saki—they are all no more
Than clay and water, phantoms without core;
    There is naught but illusion;—bring me wine
That I may leave this sea without a shore.

30

Out from my soul I came, but brought not out
The certainty I sought; I found but doubt.
    Out from my heart I went; she saw me go,
But came my love not in, nor thereabout.

31

She found me wax, she made of me, in game,
Her candle, lit it, left—but still, she came!
　When day departs, night brighter makes the fire:
O flame, devour my being, yes—but flame!

32

If words could know your loveliness, my dear,
How could they with it grow from year to year?
　Words can exalt the mole of constancy—
The mole I'll never find on you, I fear.

33

As lightly did my love abandon me
As slips the moon up from the sighing sea;
　She left without a word;—the cold moon goes,
But throws her image to her votary.

لسان الغائب خواجه شمس الدين محمد حافظ شيرازى رحمة الله عليه

34

And if a stone at my heart needs be hurled,
Yet keep the curtain to our love unfurled!
There is no need the break be heard or seen:
You'll know, I'll know—but never should the world.

35

Now I am free—I would I had my chains:
When fell the veil that hid my heart's domains
Not it alone fell down, but all the veils:
Of all that once enchanted, naught remains.

36

Come, come, I thirst, and all my gold is drowned:
Can not a buyer for this heart be found?
You say it's broken? Well, its value then
Outweighs a hundred thousand that are sound.

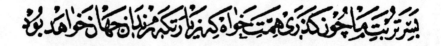

لِسَانُ الغائِبِ خواجَهُ شَمسُ الدِّينُ مُحَمَّدُ حافِظُ شِيرازِي رَحمَةُ اللهِ عَلَيهِ

37

The candle weeps; her tears are bright as dew;
She mourns the moths she's killed? That silly crew
   May so believe, but you, my son, should know
She weeps because the flame consumes her, too.

38

And He Who draws us in these flashing days,
Whom we adore, though we know whom He slays,
   He well may sorrow, for, when we are gone,
He, too, will vanish in that selfsame blaze.

39

When nears the moment when this I must die,
May old familiar wine beside me lie:
   To some friend I must then the unsaid say—
And on whom else that day may man rely?

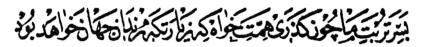

40

Why, scores of hearts do for that beggar bleed
To one that mourns the great and dead Jamshyd,
But if the beggar's wise, he'll tell you this:
Not tears of men—tears of the grape we need.

41

Shiraz, the springs of Ruknabad, the breeze
That lingers in their pleasant air—oh, these
Do not contemn, for though contemptible,
They yet adorn the world's sublimities.

42

Hafiz has never travelled far, they sneer;
What does he know? He knows be from appear:
He knows no man can go beyond his mind,
Or measure mileage of a mind that's here.

43

Where straight as suits a slave our cypress stands
And spreads his blue-black carpet, let your hands
   Arrange the cushions: Here remains Hafiz—
His glory can go out to other lands.

44

When you are here, my Love, a withered dell
Appears the garden of which Prophets tell;
   But when you're gone, then separation brings
The torture that I thought they left to Hell.

45

Svelte body of the cypress, since my side
You left, O my Beloved, I have not died:
   Ten thousand years I've lived, and through them all
In pieces slowly I have torn my pride.

46

My friends, by all that's loyal, hasten, fleet;
Go find my Love and bring me, I entreat,
   Some dust that she has trod—make no mistake:
Bring not the dust that kissed my rivals' feet.

47

The pain of love is but one tale, no more,
A hoary tale (it has been known of yore),
   Yet—strange it is—each lover that I hear
Tells me a tale I had not heard before.

48

Say day is man, and woman, pregnant night,
Say dawn is born the son of each twilight,
   Say Earth and Heaven will join, but say for me:
Enough, O Love, could our two worlds unite!

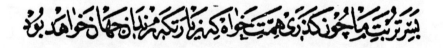

بِسَانِ الغَائِبِ خَوَاجَهُ شَمْسِ الدِّينِ مُحَمَّدِ حَافِظِ شِيرَازِي رَحْمَةُ اللهِ عَلَيهِ

49

He Who of gold and silk your tresses spun,
Who made the red rose and the white rose one
 And gave your cheek to them for honeymoon—
Can He not patience give to me, His son?

50

They say that I'm not fervid, and they lie:
If in my prayer before me there should fly
 But fleeting phantoms of your eye-brow's arch,
Why, all the temple walls would hear me sigh.

51

What alchemy is this? One glance of hers
Can wound and cure; she silhouettes and blurs
 With but one word, and when her hair I touch,
Like balm it soothes while like strong wine it stirs.

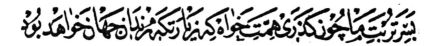

52

She said, and saying took my last defense:
Hafiz, you burn away your life to cense
   A scentless rose—no longer waste on me
The suave perfume of your intelligence.

53

Would you escape the folly of Hafiz?
Then hearken to the wind and not the breeze,
   Nor leave the road for paths where Beauty left
The imprint of her feet, or of her knees.

54

A passing breeze once sang a song to me;
I've sought it since—none knew its melody:
   Now she is gone—for her how shall I seek?
But one man knew her . . . one . . . and I am he.

55

With virgin heart I loved the fragrant pine;
Then fell the blast of lust on me, on mine;
  It passed my garden. . . . Wonder! still remained
The rose's lips, the scent of jessamine.

56

Ah, never lie upon my tomb, I pray,
Without a bowl of wine, a minstrel gay;
  My soul with life's sweet fragrance so entice
That from my grave I, too, may dance away!

57

Now! Saki, bring me now the bowl of wine!
My wisp of life let music's silk entwine!
  Today both East and West own me as lord—
Tomorrow who will know which dust is mine?

بِسَانِ الْغَائِبِ خَوَاجَهُ شَمْسُ الدِّينِ مُحَمَّدٍ حَافِظُ شِيرَازِى رَحْمَةُ اللّٰهِ عَلَيْه

58

Why should a man a towering palace raise
And with its prison walls confine my gaze?
  A shallow cave of earth has long sufficed
The proudest padishahs of other days.

59

Then by the lapwing's crown, I conjure you,
Give me to drink, though lightning sear the blue:
  Is He not as His mighty falcon proud?
And does the falcon petty prey pursue?

60

Has man the Phœnix ever made his prey?
Its name is known, and more no man can say;
  The substance lacks—so immortality:
Draw in the nets, they snare but wind and spray.

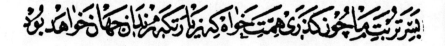

61

Who made this moor, within it left us mired,
And when His court we enter, mud-attired,
   If He can fail to pardon man, why, then,
Who has man with the love of justice fired?

62

That we may see how goes this game ignored
I'll move a pawn: behold, the wine is poured;
   I drink, and lo, the pawn makes me a King!—
Fate has no checkmate on the tavern board.

63

Unto the sober man can words reveal
This other world that drinkers see and feel?
   There is a desert and a jungle, too;
But to the desert is the jungle real?

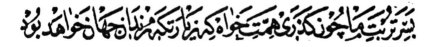

64

They closed the tavern door and turned the key,
These righteous men:—I pray to God that He
   Will not permit them now to open wide
The whited temple of hypocrisy.

65

Fret not for us, O Zahid, pure of heart;
Why should our vices make your conscience smart?
   Our page is full, but God will not ascribe
Our sins to you, though virgin be your chart.

66

Where is my turban? Head? Is this a trance?
Are these the Houris who so coyly glance?
   Have I had opium?—Nay, it is but wine
That makes the Faster with the Drunkard dance.

67

Beware, Hafiz! She has a witching eye,
And not to Heaven do the witches fly:
 Deceit's their trade—from such an eye springs love
As from a stone sparks flash and, flashing, die.

68

Needs love a sword? With but one look she can
Take half my life, and stay beyond the ban;
 Ah, if I met my Love a thousand times,
Each time her eyes would say: Who is this man?

69

What though she plight her hand, or plight her glove,
Though we be one, or two, though crow and dove,
 Sweet may the bitter to the bitter be—
I thirst for pain: I am in love with love.

70

Yet, but to know one hour's full repose!
Upon this sour-faced world a door to close!
  Here, Magi! pour us of the wine that brings
An instant's peace—an hour's no one knows.

71

When Winter mourns his dead, his melting rain
Of tears awakes the soil; from buried grain
  The rose returns, from dust life springs anew:
Why then in earth, O Love, must you remain?

72

I sowed some seeds (the dealer called them wheat),
I sowed those seeds (no others, I repeat),
  Yet when I reaped and to the market came,
The selfsame dealer said my crop was cheat.

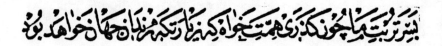

73

Then spoke a peasant to his son, half-grown:—
For you but this I ask at Allah's throne:
  May you sow only that which you would reap,
And reap then only that which you have sown.

74

The gold in this world's market, and its price
In pain, behold, and choose your paradise;
  If golden profit be for you enough,
For us the loss of pain will quite suffice.

75

The face of God to many is a sign
Of beauty endless as a circled line;
  I, too, might find it so, if there I saw
But one small grain of constancy divine.

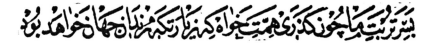

76

The horse of life brings every man where hides
Vicissitude; each senses ill betides:
  But I, says each, shall not his captive fall!—
And straight the horseman in the ambush rides.

77

Yet though through life man trembles on a hair
With but his mind to right him—let him dare
  To balance with it in the ebon void,
And Fate shall be the one who shall despair.

78

I do exist—when I myself ignore?
I don't exist—and yet knock at this door?
  Hafiz! Keep back your subtleties like gold:
The mint is our false coiner—say no more.

79

To find the meanings that my lines bestow,
Waste not your wit, nor say: It's thus and so.
   This pen you need not hope to understand—
Not even I will all its secrets know.

80

I ask no word about the how and why,
A slave, I do as may the master cry.—
   Who told you then that I think still of you?
O my Beloved, I tell you, it's a lie!

81

Some by their thoughts would paradise acquire,
While I with mine would feed her memory's fire:
   So are the thoughts wrought in the minds of men
Shaped to the market of each man's desire.

بِسَانِ الْغَائِبِ خَوَاجَهُ شَمْسِ الدِّينِ مَحَمَّدٍ حَافِظ شِيرَازِى رَحْمَةُ اللهِ عَلَيْهِ

82

You sigh that you were not of Fortune blest?
From you she turned her face? But did you rest
　Before her door awhile? Enough to see
How in the end she poisons every guest?

83

Through my declining years companions three
Have loyal stayed: the first one, poverty;
　The second, solitude; the third is pain;—
But stay! A fourth fills one small cup for me!

84

Wait, wait, my lass! Pour out your wine again,
Two cups—or three—for each of all these men
　Who say that they abjure the merry life;—
Should they refuse, why, I will drink them then.

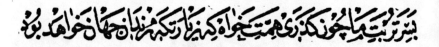

85

Spurn not my wine, nor spend your life in dread
Of what about you is or will be said;
   Posterity? Of you what will it say
Except, perhaps: God keep him—he is dead.

86

Assay this dust as in a treasure mine:
Here's Life, here's Death, the fertile, the malign;
   Here are the lip and cup at last made one—
No more, alas, the drinker and the wine.

87

Unto the ignorant God gives a rein
To their desires: His Heaven they'll attain;
   But you are skilled in thinking, you are wise:
That sin suffices for eternal pain.

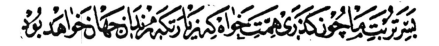

88

A sage replied: A wise man never racks
His mind for secrets that no vintner lacks:
Hold nothing serious in this world, my friend,
For life loads down the men who bend their backs.

89

Then, offering me from out the sparkling bowl:
Take life as wine, he said, it too is droll;
Live with a smile although your heart may bleed;—
Not moans but lutes should bare the wounded soul.

90

Man is a marvel by a Marvel planned
Not to reply, but answers to demand;
He is allowed to hear the Voice, and know
There is one tongue he shall not understand.

91

Then, Magi, wine! and wine of noble race!
What matter if my folly grow apace?
    The Lord of Folly—He will understand,
He will forgive, and He can all efface!

92

Speak not of shame, I pray, it is my name,
The ever-flowing source of all my fame;
    Nor talk of reputation, for, my friend,
From my renown has come my deepest shame.

93

All unaware, Hafiz, you came to dwell
Within this house of life; and now to Hell
    They say you must at any moment go:
Well, as you leave, sing life a brave farewell!

بِسَانِ الْغَائِبِ خَوَاجَهُ شَمْسِ الدِّينِ مُحَمَّد حَافِظ شِيرَازِي رَحْمَةُ اللهِ عَلَيْهِ

94

Though sin we did not choose, no more than wine
Chose from the grape to come, yet do not whine:
   Strive still to be, Hafiz, the gentleman!
When He reproaches, say: The sin is mine.

95

My life is spent; it was a precious sum
Spent like an arrow for the bow's short thrum.
   An arrow sped does not return; but oh,
Come back, my Love, and back my life will come!

96

No monumental tomb do I require,
But place me where some cypress will not tire
   His cooling shadow evermore to throw
Upon the burning dust of my desire.

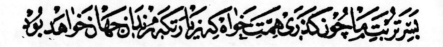

97

Though I in Hell pay for my liberties,
While wine and tavern are, and maidens please,
    There even shall the timid turn to soothe
A thirst born of the dust that was Hafiz.

98

Immortal Daughter of the Vine, when you
Come to my tomb to serve the motley crew
    Of joyous pilgrims drawn to my Divan,
Ask grace for old Hafiz—he sins anew.

99

O God of men, why hold concealed Your light?
When shall Your sun erase this blot of night?
    Can You not spare us but one flash, one beam?
Must we believe that You are in our plight?

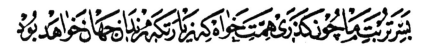

100

Then from the fragile table seize a tass
And drain the wine of life before the glass
  Shall crumbling fall, with table and with you,
And with your God into oblivion pass.

101

But ere you free the glass from all its wine
And through its crystal see a new world shine,
  Throw some to those who knew that magic, too,
And cool the wind—the wind's their drink, and mine.

EPILOGUE

If I stay on as yonder gnarlèd trunk,
The sap all gone (in wine that we have drunk),
   Spared by the very wounds that begged the axe
As each of them into its body sunk:

If I live on until desire is dead,
Mayhap then I'll recant all I have said;
   But if I do, do you remember still:
No vine is fertile when the sap has fled.

HAFIZ

HAFIZ, during his lifetime, was famed not only in his own Persia but far beyond its borders. Since his death that fame has grown and spread with the centuries. Yet very little is known about his life.

His real name was Shams-ud-Din Mohammed. To this foundation several additions have been made. He added one himself when, in accordance with the custom of the times, he adopted a *takhallus*, or pen name, which has made him known to posterity as Hafiz. (The word in Persian means either "a care-taker" or, more usually, "one who remembers," and is generally applied to those who know the Koran by heart.) The love his fellows had for him then gave him the title of *Khajeh*, the "old master" or the "teacher," while local pride joined to the whole the word *Shiraz-i*, "of Shiraz," the city where he was born, lived and is buried. His full name among the Persians is thus Khajeh Shams-ud-Din Mohammed Hafiz Shiraz-i.

Hafiz was born in the early fourteenth century, a decade or so after the death of Saadi, and some three hundred years after that of Firdausi—the two writers whom the Persians generally class with Hafiz as their three greatest poets. He died near the end of the century. It would no doubt please Hafiz's keen sense of the ironic to know that, although his works are read now in tongues of which he never heard, neither the time of his entry in nor of his departure from the world is recorded as certainly as that of shahs whose names and reigns are otherwise forgotten.

Shiraz, which gave the world both Hafiz and Saadi, is said to have been founded in 697 A.D. It is now the capital of the province that the Persians call Fars. Fars is a Moslem name for all Persia. It was in Fars that the mighty Persian empire of classic history arose. Only some thirty leagues from Shiraz are the impressive remains of Persepolis, more than 1,700 years old even when Hafiz knew them. Among them are the ruins that the Persians have long called the Throne of Jamshyd and the Throne of Kaikhosru*, those legendary kings to the passing of whose glory both Omar and Hafiz loved to point.

That glory had indeed passed when this nucleus of never-dying Persia produced the "most Persian of the Persian" poets. Even that fragment of the empire of Darius which is Persia to our maps, was then divided into

---

* Jamshyd, according to the *Shah Namah*, Firdausi's celebrated Book of Kings, was the fourth king of Persia. He is supposed to have reigned seven hundred years and during that time to have founded Persepolis, subdued the entire universe (including the demons, fairies and birds), and to have divided mankind into four classes in this rank: priests and savants; warriors; farmers; and business men "whose spirit is forever troubled." To Jamshyd are attributed the discovery of all the precious stones, the first pearl fisheries and the first baths, the invention of iron weapons, armour, medicine, and bricks, and the art of making perfume. Jamshyd (or Jam or Djemschid) corresponds to the mythical Yima of the *Avesta*, or the Yama of the *Veda*. Kaikhosru, the great-grandson of Kaikobad and the twelfth legendary king, reigned during the old age of the Rustem of Arnold's poem.

a number of petty Moslem kingdoms, with Shiraz as the capital of the Shah of Fars. It was a time of tumult, politically, at least, and of wars among the neighbouring Shahs, while from the North the shadow and then the substance of the power of Timur spread over all the land.

Shiraz, however, seems to have enjoyed in this period a prosperity that did not really decline until three hundred years later. Earthquakes in the early nineteenth century helped to achieve its ruin, destroying most of the baths, mosques, and colleges that then remained. The present rebuilt (if not "modern") city of some 50,000 inhabitants is not the Shiraz that Hafiz loved. But it is still known for its wine, our dictionaries defining the English word, Shiraz, as "a rich sweet wine, either red or white," resembling Tokay in taste.

If Shiraz knows decay now, it knew a high state of culture and civilization when illiteracy was still high among the rulers of our ancestors in Europe. One of the few things about Hafiz of which we are certain is that he received an excellent education and was as well versed in the Arabic as in the Persian tongue.

He did not live, however, in a biographical age. At least, no life of Hafiz, written in his own time, has come down to us. About the only reliable contemporary reference to it that we have is a brief passage written by Muhammad Gulandam, a pupil of Hafiz to whom some attribute the first collection of his works, although others credit this to another pupil, Syed Kasim-al-Anwar. In the preface to his Divan* of Hafiz, Muhammad Gulan-

---

* *Divan* in Persian means a collection of poems. It also means a court, a place where judgment is passed.

dam pays tribute to the poet's "incomparable genius, his catholic sympathy and the celebrity attained by his verse even in his lifetime, not only in Persia from Fars to Khurasan and Azerbaijan, but in India, Turkestan and Mesopotamia," and he then adds:

> However, diligent study of the Koran, constant attendance to the King's business, the annotation of the *Kashshaf* [a commentary of the Koran] and the *Misbah,* the perusal of the *Matali* and the *Miftah* [all books of the thirteenth century], the acquisition of canons of literary criticism and the appreciation of Arabic poems prevented him from collecting his verses and *ghazals,* or editing and arranging his poems.
>
> The writer of these lines, this least of men, Muhammad Gulandam, when he was attending the lectures of our Master, that most eminent teacher, Qiwamu'd-Din 'Abdullah, used constantly and repeatedly to urge, in the course of conversation, that he (Hafiz) should gather together all these rare gems in one concatenation and assemble all these lustrous pearls on one string, so that they might become a necklace of great price for his contemporaries or a girdle for the brides of his time.
>
> With this request, however, he was unable to comply, alleging lack of appreciation on the part of his contemporaries as an excuse, until he bade farewell to this life.*

There are, of course, biographies of Hafiz written in later times and in many languages, but they conflict bewilderingly on nearly every point. Some say Hafiz was born of a good family. Others say that he was of obscure origin, specifying even that his father was a baker of Shiraz. One source rather combines the two, stating that the father of Hafiz was Baha-ud-Din, who migrated from Ispahan to Shiraz in the time of the Atabeks of Fars, became rich there in commerce and died leaving his

* EDWARD G. BROWNE: *A History of Persian Literature under Tartar Dominion* (A.D. 1265-1502). Cambridge University Press, 1920.

wife and their small son, the poet, in such poverty that the boy had to work for his living.

According to one widely repeated tale, the boy had an uncle, Sadi, who one day began composing a *ghazal* on the Sufi philosophy. Interrupted after he had written but the first line of the poem, he returned to find that Hafiz had completed the couplet. Sadi, struck by the genius of his nephew, told him to finish the *ghazal*. When it was done, he cursed him, saying: "Your poetry shall bring the curse of insanity on the reader." There are still those who believe that the works of Hafiz have this effect.

Whether Hafiz took his pen name at the early age at which he seems to have started writing poetry, or whether he got it from learning the Koran by heart in school, can not be said. There is no doubt, however, that Hafiz was as familiar with that often majestic poem of the Prophet as his name indicates. He is said to have written a commentary on it and to have been a professor of Moslem theology, skilled also in jurisprudence. (The two go together in Islam, where the Koran is at once the spiritual and the temporal law.) He appears, indeed, to have been widely famed as a teacher. It is related that the vizir, Kawam-ud-Din, founded not merely a chair, but a college for him.

While some accounts picture Hafiz as an austere man who embraced poverty and was devoted to the Moslem religion, others represent him as one who was given to dissipation* and conviviality, and who lived that life of pleasure which the Persians long before had developed to

* It should be remarked that pious Moslems, whose religion forbids all alcoholic liquors, frequently style a man a drunkard and debauchee if he drinks wine at all, no matter how moderately.

the point where it gave the Prophet his conception of paradise. Persian paintings, it may be noted, sometimes depict Hafiz as a youth of surpassing beauty. None of these are contemporary, however, and I know of no physical description of the poet.

Those who would make Hafiz out as a most respectable citizen add that he had a wife and one or more children, all of whom he dearly loved and all of whom preceded him to the grave. They hold that certain *ghazals* are addressed to his wife, and that certain fragments were written on the death of his son or sons. But all this is open to question. Considering the extreme privacy that surrounds family life among the Moslems, one could hardly expect to find much authentic information on that of Hafiz. Certainly some of his poems are addressed or refer to women other than his wife, such as the "lovely Turk of Shiraz," and Shakh-i-Nabat, the Branch of Sugar Cane. Judging from his *ghazals* he had many loves, but he rarely mentions any of them by name.

The version that fits in best with the Hafiz whom his Divan reveals to me relates that he was early taught to despise neither the physical world nor the world of the spirit or intellect. As a youth, it says, he studied under an eminent Sufi, Sheikh Mohammad Attar, who, though classed as a mystic, was by no means an ascetic. The Sheikh, indeed, seems to have combined the teaching of philosophy with earning a more certain livelihood by running a small green-grocery business, which appears to have allowed him both sufficient time and money to frequent the tavern. His practice did not differ from his teaching, for he taught that one should not neglect the body or the mind. This creed, or perhaps his application of it, outraged the more orthodox Sufis, but the Divan would indicate that he won the adherence of his distinguished pupil.

The poems of Hafiz, however, yield surprisingly little information about his life or his times. There are casual allusions, of course, but from reading them alone, as Gertrude Lowthian Bell has brilliantly shown, one would hardly divine that Shiraz, while Hafiz lived there, was besieged and captured half a dozen times, passing swiftly from a reign of revelry to a reign of terror and bigotry, then back to ribaldry followed by more bloodshed, until in their rapid succession its petty Shahs passed from independent monarchs to tributary vassals of Timur, and then completely under his dominion.

The very rareness of even oblique reference to all this in the poems of Hafiz in itself portrays the man. It was as unimportant to him then as it is to us now. He was a man who on the spot could give the verdict of posterity. Miss Bell contrasts Dante with his contemporary, Hafiz: the Italian closely reflecting his time; the Persian with a horizon that disdained contemporary history as too fragmentary an episode to occupy his thoughts. She says of Hafiz:

"It is as if his mental eye, endowed with wonderful acuteness of vision, had penetrated into those provinces of thought which we of a later age were destined to inhabit."*

As every age since the fourteenth century, however,

---

* The whole of the preface to Gertrude Bell's *Poems from the Divan of Hafiz* (London: Heinemann, 1897), from which this is taken, is warmly recommended, as well as her translations of selected *ghazals*.

has passed much the same judgment on Hafiz, it is, perhaps, premature even now to suggest that we, at last, live in the world the Persian poet knew.

If Hafiz neglected his Shahs, there were many others who did not. A glance at their history will throw some light on the poet. The first Shah of Shiraz whom Hafiz knew was fortunately Abu Ishak Inju, a pleasure-loving prince, a poet himself and a friend of poets. His successor in 1353, Mubariz-ud-Din Muhammad Muzaffar, was the opposite of his victim.

"Harsh, stern and ascetic in character, he had no sooner taken possession of Shiraz than he caused all the taverns to be closed and put a stop, as far as possible, to the drinking of wine, to the great annoyance of Hafiz."

Indeed, there are more references to this prohibition era in the Divan than to any other one event, a fact which does little to support the thesis that Hafiz was an austere mystic. Professor Browne,* to whom I am indebted for the quotation, goes on to translate some of the poems in which Hafiz, with surprising boldness for a subject of so bloodthirsty a Puritan as this Shah, reveals his annoyance:

> Though wine gives delight and the wind distils the perfume
> of the rose,
> Drink not wine to the strains of the harp, for the constable
> is alert.
> Hide the goblet in the sleeve of the patchwork cloak,
> For the time, like the eye of the decanter, pours forth blood.
> Wash your dervish-cloak from the wine-stain with tears,
> For it is the season of piety and the time of abstinence.

* *Op. cit.* All five of the translations that follow are by Professor Browne

Hafiz, who in his poems nearly always scorned the "modern instance" as too trivial, did not scorn the one that was to be considered later as a most modern departure. He wrote for the fourteenth and the twentieth centuries:

O will it be that they will reopen the doors of the taverns,
And will loosen the knots from our tangled affairs?
Cut the tresses of the harp (in mourning) for the death of pure wine,
So that all the sons of the Magians may loosen their curled locks!
Write the letter of condolence for the (death of the) Daughter of the Grape,
So that all the comrades may let loose blood (-stained tears) from their eye-lashes.
They have closed the doors of the wine-taverns; O God, suffer not
That they should open the doors of the house of deceit and hypocrisy!*
If they have closed them for the sake of the heart of the self righteous zealot,
Be of good heart, for they will reopen them for God's sake!

The Shah's son, happily, agreed with Hafiz, and himself left this quatrain to a world of which he never dreamed:

In the assembly of the time the concomitants of wine-bibbing are laid low;
Neither is the hand on the harp, nor the tambourine in the hand.

---

* This is the original of *rubai* 64. The Magians (or Magis) referred to in the above *ghazal* were the remnants of the followers of Zoroaster, whose religion did not forbid wine as Islam does. They kept most of the taverns of the time in Persia.

All the revellers have abandoned the worship of wine,
Save the city constable, who is drunk without wine.

This prince in 1357 succeeded his father, who, never
having heard of Constitutions, had not thought of the
device of a constitutional amendment for perpetuating
his bigotry. Shah Shuja consequently had no difficulty in
ending at once the dry regime of his parent. Hafiz hailed
Shuja as the re-opener of the tavern:

At early Dawn good tidings reached my ear from the Unseen
Voice:
"It is the era of Shah Shuja: drink wine boldly!"
That time is gone when men of insight went apart
With a thousand words in the mouth but their lips silent.
To the sound of the harp we will tell those stories
At the hearing of which the cauldron of our bosoms boiled.
Princes (alone) know the secrets of their kingdom;
O Hafiz, thou art a beggarly recluse; hold thy peace!

His joy could not be confined to a single poem, and he
wrote again:

The harp began to clamour "Where is the objector?"
The cup began to laugh "Where is the forbidder?"
Pray for the King's long life if thou seekest the world's welfare,
For he is a beneficent being and a generous benefactor,
The manifestation of Eternal Grace, the Light of the Eye of
Hope,
The combiner of theory and practice, the Life of the World,
Shah Shuja.

Although Hafiz and Shah Shuja were in perfect accord
on this subject which both held so important, their rela-
tions were not very happy. While the Shah was a poet,

he was not a friend of poets, especially those who were more famed than he.

Shah Shuja was followed in 1383 by his son, who was imprisoned by his cousin, Shah Mansur, in 1387. But the deposed Shah had accepted the suzerainty of Timur and that redoubtable warrior entered Shiraz before the year was out. Timur not only had an account to settle with Mansur, but, it appears, with Hafiz as well.

Tradition relates that the already celebrated couplet (given as my *rubái* 19), in which Hafiz offered the cities of Boukhara and Samarkand for the mole on the cheek of his Turkish mistress, had mightily displeased the man who, starting with those two cities, had made much of the world pay them tribute. He had the poet, then near his deathbed (already dead, by some chronologies) brought before him. The story of their meeting might be almost literally given thus in *rubái* form, put into the mouth of Hafiz:

> My verses roused the conquering Timur's ire:
> Did you, he glared, thus give my cities?—Sire,
>   It's true, I said, and by such reckless gifts
> Impoverished now, your largess I require.

The reply, at least typical of the quick wit that all anecdotes about Hafiz ascribe to him, is said to have so pleased Timur that he rewarded the poet he had intended to punish.

Other rulers far from Shiraz had already honoured Hafiz. He received many invitations to visit distant courts, but nearly always he refused to leave Shiraz, a city for which he expressed his love in several poems.

There appears to be only one accepted record of his ever having left it. His admirer, Mahmud Shah Bahmani, sent funds to Hafiz to bring him to his capital in India. Hafiz spent most of the money before leaving Shiraz. The rest went when, on the short trip to the Persian Gulf, he met a penniless friend at Lar. Two Persian merchants, who were also admirers of Hafiz, happened to be in Lar en route to India and they then offered to pay the poet's expenses on the trip. Hafiz went with them to the Gulf, but when they embarked a storm arose which so frightened him that he at once put back to shore. He returned to Shiraz and in a poem proclaimed that a hundred jewels could not induce him to sail again. The couplet from *ghazal* 13 (in *Alif*) which inspired my *rubái* 42, bears out the belief that Hafiz was not given to travel.

The Divan of Hafiz, as edited in the seventeenth century by Sudi, the Turk who has since been recognized as the poet's greatest commentator, contains 573 *ghazals*, to which are also attached 69 *rubáiyát*, 42 fragments and 9 miscellaneous poems. There are many other texts of the Divan in Persian, some giving an even greater number of *ghazals*. While Hafiz did not invent the *ghazal*, he did much to improve and perfect it as a Persian verse form. Frequently he even took couplets from other poets, his predecessors or contemporaries, and rewrote them merely to bring out better the beauty he saw in them. The Persians did not consider this plagiarism.

As for his style, Sir Gore Ouseley expressed the views of many other critics, in Persia and elsewhere, when he described it as "displaying at the same time great learning, matured science and intimate knowledge of the hidden as well as the apparent nature of things, but above all a certain fascination of expression unequalled by any other poet."

The agreement on the beauty of his style does not, however, extend to the philosophy Hafiz expressed with it. The dispute here is so sharp that diametrically opposed schools, as the Sufi mystics and the hedonists, both claim him as their own.

Such great Sufi philosophers as the Persian poet, Jami, judge Hafiz from his verses to have been "a Sufi of eminence." The Sufis have a very complete and ingenious code whereby they use sensuous words and images to convey their hidden mystic thought. Thus *wine* by this Sufi code represents *spiritual ecstasy*, the *beloved* is the *Divinity*, the *tavern* is the *Sufi monastery*, the *Magi* or tavern keeper is the *spiritual guide*, and so on into more abstract terms. Those who consider Hafiz a Sufi mystic explain his verse by this code, and it is obvious that, if one is sufficiently zealous, much of the Divan can be interpreted in this way.*

Other Persians, however, criticize Hafiz for certain verses that express fatalism, a doctrine of the orthodox or *Sunni* Moslems which is abhorred by the *Shiah* sect of

---

* Those who seek the mystical interpretation of Hafiz will find it in the prose translation by H. Wilberforce Clarke (*Hafiz, The Divan*, 2 v. Government of India Printing Office, 1891). He not only adds the mystical meaning in parentheses after the literal rendition, but even in his choice of the literal word he leans strongly to the mystical school. Here, as a typical instance, is the way in which Clarke gives the stanza of *ghazal* 15 (in *Alif*) which inspired my *rubái* 12:

O my soul! if our Bold One (the Beloved) practise profligacy (sincerity and oneness), and intoxication (disregard),—

First, it is proper to abandon chastity (devotion) and austerity (abstinence).

Islam to which the Persians belong. In particular they point to the couplet that can be given thus as a *rubái*:

> Long Fate has kept me waiting at her door,
> Receiving others, though I came before;
> You find me now unpleasing?—Can you change
> The heart of Kismet then? I ask no more.

Still other Persians agree with Von Hammer, who, punning on the Arabic meaning of Hafiz's name, *Shams-ud-Din*, said: "*The Sun of the Faith* cast but an uncertain light, and the Interpreter of Secrets [a title given Hafiz by his mystic admirers] interpreted only the language of pleasure."

For my part, I would give Hafiz no label. The genius is a school in himself.

The confusion among those who would classify Hafiz arises from his giving the stamp of his personality to various doctrines, each of which makes up the complete philosophy of smaller men. He shared some of the views of some Sufis, of some fatalists, of some hedonists. He impresses me as one who completed the Delphic injunction to make it read: "Moderation in all things—even in moderation."

We must remember, too, that the Divan, which comes to us as a whole, was not written as a single book, a fact that seems to have escaped those who would pin Hafiz down to some one school and explain away all conflicts in the text. The poems in the Divan were written over a period covering nearly a century, and, unfortunately, we have no data for arranging them chronologically. We can certainly assume that the views of Hafiz changed and developed during his long life and that these changes are reflected in his poems, even though we can not trace them. And even if we could, it would not necessarily follow that the last poems he wrote represent him more truly than others do. I have long been unable to feel the weight that many attach, for instance, to recantations made by atheists on their deathbeds, or in their second childhood. The fresh vision of the first childhood, usually dismissed as puerile, may be at least as profound.

Hafiz, I would agree, was strongly influenced by the Sufi doctrine in its broadest application. But merely to call a man a Sufi is to say little, for Sufis have differed so much in degree as to differ in kind. The confusion about what Sufism means extends even to its origin.

Some say it was an independent growth. Others hold that it represents the "esoteric Islam," a secret doctrine first propagated among the elect by Ali, the son-in-law of the Prophet. Still others trace it to Plato and the Greeks. They point out that three great Sufi teachers flourished in the time of the Arabian Nights, when the scholars of Harun-al-Rashid and other great Caliphs were translating the Hellenic philosophers and starting them on their long pilgrimage from Bagdad around the North Coast of Africa to Moorish Spain and thus back, in re-translation from the Arabic, to the renascent West, which in its barbaric interlude had lost or destroyed many of the originals.

The basic principle of Sufism is the oneness of Man and the Divinity, but that principle is so prolific as to give birth to many doctrines which, like children, diverge more and more not only from their parent but also from their brothers. Thus some may emphasize, in the Sufi union, the Divinity, and throw free will to the winds, while others may stress Man and either deduct that Man is not only his own master but his own God, or at least approach fatalism from an entirely different angle.

Thus, Hadaj, in the ninth century, boldly declared: "I am God,"—and for his boldness was put to horrible death by the orthodox Moslems. Many of the stanzas of Hafiz reveal this same basic belief. Indeed, in at least one of them he seems to refer directly to the celebrated Hadaj, saying that the "fools whom God has not inspired can not know the meaning of him who said: 'I am God.' "

Some of those whom the Persians class as Sufis were developing the philosophies of modern Europe when metaphysical thinking was not done among the best circles in the West. Syed Abdul Majid* points out that the Cartesian doctrine of dualism was "propounded by the great Sufi Alghazali long before Descartes—that is to say, the existence of mind and matter with the pineal gland— with the addition of Malebranche's doctrine of Occasionalism for Descartes' pineal gland." The stanza of Hafiz from which my *rubái 77* is taken puts the same emphasis on the mind as man's only guide that led Descartes to make *tabula rasa* of all his unconsciously acquired mental baggage and thus reach his formula: I think, therefore I am. Hafiz, it seems to me, went even further along the same route in the lines that I give as *rubái 78*.

One of the practices that the great Sufis seem to

---

* In the introduction and appendix to his English translation of *The Rubáiyát of Hafiz* (London: John Murray, 1919, with a verse rendition by L. Cranmer-Byng) Syed Abdul Majid also shows the affinity of various Sufi schools to Locke, Berkeley, Leibnitz and Kant, respectively.

have shared, however much they differed in theory, was that of tolerance. In an age of religious fanaticism it mattered nothing to them whether a man was a Moslem, a Christian or a Jew. Hafiz had the same quality. More than five hundred years ago he could express this view (which does not seem yet to be that of western Christians even in relief work in regions where both Christians and Moslems are afflicted by disaster):

O zealot, think not that you are sheltered from the sins of pride,
For the difference between the mosque and the church of the infidel is but vanity.

Broad as the basic Sufi doctrine is, the name itself is generally associated with those whom it has led to mysticism and ascetism. I can not subscribe to the beliefs that Hafiz was a Sufi of this variety, or that he was a pious Moslem. The *ghazals* that prohibition in Shiraz inspired him to write, to mention but them, do not paint their author even as an orthodox Mohammedan, let alone an ascetic. Those who interpret Hafiz with the mystic Sufi code-book in hand usually admit that they themselves find it inadequate for all his sensual images. To say that much of the Divan *may be* interpreted mystically is simply to admit that it has another sense which requires no such effort to be understood. And since all of it can not possibly be rendered allegorically, it is plain that the hedonistic philosophy was at least shared by Hafiz.

Further evidence that Hafiz was not a mystic lies in the fact (at least, it is as well established as anything about the life of Hafiz) that the religious interpretation of his verses was disputed even in Shiraz in his own day. Had Hafiz meant his poems to be taken in a religous sense, it was in his interest, considering the time in which he lived and the fanaticism of the orthodox, to have written them in unmistakably religious terms, or at least to have left no doubt of their being allegorical.

Instead, the evidence is that he had to take care, as Descartes* did, to protect himself and his doctrines by soothing the Jesuits of the day. Shah Shuja (perhaps more from jealousy than piety) found the final couplet of *ghazal* 525 (in *Ya*) so heretical that he had Hafiz hailed before the theological doctors of Shiraz, whose ire he hoped to raise against the author. There was no saving mystical interpretation that could be given to this stanza. But let Syed Abdul Majid, a Persian who himself prefers to interpret Hafiz mystically, tell the rest of the story:

> Fortunately for the poet, he came to know of it before they [the theologians] sat in judgment over his lines and his fate. He at once added a line putting it into the mouth of a Christian, there being no harm in a Christian calling in question the faith of Hafiz. The decision was a foregone conclusion. Hafiz was acquitted and Shah was censured for his groundless accusation.

What the theological judges read was this (the last two lines remaining as they stood when they roused the Shah):

> How pleasantly to me came this tale, when, in the early morning,
> At the door of the wine house, with drum and reed, a Christian said:—

---

* Descartes had for device: *bene vixit, bene qui latuit* (to live happily, live hidden). He was a "hero," as Hegel has said, only in his speculative life.

66

If being a Moslem [the Arabic word, *Muslim*, means "one who submits himself to God"] is to be of the sort that Hafiz is— Alas, if after today there should be a tomorrow.

No one was likely to feel the irony of Hafiz being saved by his "context" more than Shah Shuja himself. For the Shah had once sharply criticized Hafiz for the utter incoherency of his poems, saying: "In one and the same *ghazal* you write of wine, of Sufism and of your loves."

To this Hafiz is said to have replied: "It is true, and yet everyone knows, admires and repeats my verses, while those of some poets I might name do not seem to go beyond the city gates."

Some, indeed, attribute the heresy charge to the poet-Shah's anger at this retort.

More than once quick wit saved Hafiz. The opening line of his *ghazal* in *Alif,** which is generally placed as the first one in the Divan, he took from a couplet written by Caliph Yazid. This was not considered plagiarism by the Persians, but it was considered most audacious daring. The name of Yazid was never mentioned by pious Persians any more then than it is now without the imprecation, *La-nat-ul-lah!*—be accursed of God!

The horror that any reference to Yazid inspires in them is not because this early successor of the Prophet is

---

* My *rubái* 24 is drawn from the first stanza of this *ghazal,* which can be given thus in prose:

O cup-bearer, pass around the bowl of vision-giving wine;

For love seemed an easy precept for us to follow, but what difficulties it presents!

The couplet of Yazid ran:

I am poisoned and I have with me neither the antidote nor him that by magic cures poison:

O cup-bearer, pass around the bowl of wine of love.

supposed to have been a drunkard and an atheist, but because he attempted to poison Husain, the grandson of the Prophet, and, failing in this, slew him and all his family on the plains of Kerbela. Now Husain and Hasan, together with their father, Ali, are the only successors of the Prophet that the Persians recognize as legitimate. Indeed, the Shiah sect was founded mainly on loyalty to the unfortunate house of Ali. The anniversary of the martyrdom of Husain is celebrated every year by the Persians. His death at the hands of Yazid is kept alive to this day in a miracle play given during the ten days the anniversary ceremonies last, fanatical enthusiasm at that time reaching an extraordinary pitch.

It was this Yazid of anathema whose lines Hafiz blandly incorporated into Persian verse. He was very soon asked how he came thus to "borrow from Yazid, a usurper and the murderer of Imam Husain, son of Ali." Hafiz turned wrath away with this reply:

> Which of you, seeing a dog running away with a diamond,
> would not stop him and take the jewel from his unclean mouth?

Yet, despite his wit, his subterfuges and the possibility he gave of mystical interpretation to much of his verse, when the works of Hafiz were collected in the Divan after his death, attempts were made, it is related, to prevent the publication of the book, on the ground that it was too heretical to be allowed general circulation. The enemies of Hafiz denounced him among other things for praising the wine which the Prophet had forbidden. His friends explained that his wine and his mistresses were merely Sufi symbols of the Divinity.

Fortunately for posterity, the fate of the Divan was referred to Abu Suoud, an eminent Sufi and apparently a member of its broadest school. With a common sense that is all too uncommon Abu Suoud ruled that "everyone was at liberty to use his own judgment in the meaning he ascribed to the poems of Hafiz."

It would seem from all this that the "mysticism" of Hafiz was simply a protective covering he adopted, or one that was put forward by his friends to save his works.* Nor should it be surprising to see even Moslem theologians upholding such religious interpretations of Hafiz. The Church everywhere has frequently converted to her own purposes what she once called the works of the devil. Moreover, some Persian theologians may have shared in secret the ideas of Hafiz, or they may have been like the French royalists and reactionaries who denounce the radical doctrines of Anatole France but are so enthralled by his art that they would not suppress a book of his.

To show where mystical interpretations may lead one, I have written two *rubáiyát* from one verse. Literally translated in prose it would be:

The face of my love is ravishing.
It would be perfect if I could see on her cheek the beauty spot that is the emblem of fidelity.

* I find my view is one that Renan has already given. In discussing the similarly allegorical interpretation of the Biblical Song of Songs, he goes into the general question, in his *Cantique des Cantiques*, and says: "*Pour Hafiz, par exemple, il semble bien que l'explication allégorique est le plus souvent un fruit de la fantaisie des commentateurs, ou des précautions que les admirateurs du poëte étaient obligés de prendre pour sauver l'orthodoxie de leur auteur favori.*"

69

Taking this literally, I wrote *rubái* 32. Interpreting "love" allegorically as the Divinity, I wrote *rubái* 75, and it is, I fear, the "mystical" one which would please the good Moslem the least.

Perhaps Hafiz meant the stanza both ways. Certainly his poems are filled with hidden meanings and many of his verses lend themselves more easily to two or even more interpretations than does this particular couplet. I have tried in my *rubáiyát* to retain this style, frugal of words and fruitful of meaning, for it is a very distinctive characteristic of the poetry of Hafiz.

Indeed, if Hafiz hinted at the Sufi mystical code as a camouflage for some of his hedonism, it is quite possible that at other times he veiled speculation on the Divinity not only by putting it in the mouths of Christians but also by clothing it in superficially innocent phrases. Thus the lines that inspired *rubái* 37 seemed to me to carry with them a wider implication which I put into *rubái* 38.

The real reason why Hafiz never collected his poems may well have been this same necessity for prudence, rather than the explanation, "lack of appreciation," which Muhammad Gulandam ascribes to him. The danger such a project involved for him was shown quite plainly in the dispute that arose over the collection of his works after his death. It is improbable that Hafiz did not realize that the heresy he scatters in disguises of all sorts or in small doses through his *ghazals* would have a much stronger effect when his works were all assembled than they had when the poems were read separately. One suspects that Hafiz felt as did Anatole France, whom M. Brousson reports as saying:

Certain truths particularly hard for hierarchies, established order, common sense—one must present them with extreme non-chalance. We labour for the bourgeois clientèle. It is the only one that reads. Do not tear away the veil from the temple with a brutal hand. Crumple it. Riddle it with little unseen holes. Under pretext of mending it, cut off, here and there, some ragged edges to make dolls with them. Leave to your reader the easy victory of seeing further than you do. . . .

I am taken for a jester, for a juggler, for a sophist. . . . I have spent my life in wrapping dynamite in little fancy papers."

Anatole France lived in such times that the State which he ridiculed gave him a magnificent funeral when he died. But Hafiz, even though his poems were not available in cumulative form, was considered such a heretic that, when he died, his body was refused a Moslem religious burial. After a long dispute between the friends and the enemies of the poet, says Sher Khan Lodi in his memoirs, they finally agreed to let the question be decided by appeal to Hafiz himself. Several *ghazals* in his handwriting were placed in an urn. The verse drawn out was from *ghazal* 60 (in *Ta*) and it read:

Passer-by, turn not from the grave of Hafiz:
Though soiled by sin, perhaps he has been welcomed in Paradise.

He was then buried with all the religious rites. "It is a fortunate age," as Miss Bell says, "which will allow a man's writings to stand his doubtful reputation in such good stead."

It may be that from this incident arose the practice, still widely prevalent in the East (and even among Moslems in America) of divining from the Divan of Hafiz. As our medieval ancestors, to whom Virgil was a wizard, used his *Æneid* as a key to the future, so Easterners have long opened the Divan of Hafiz at random and guided their action by the *ghazal,* or its "master verse," which they thus found. They have, indeed, evolved the most intricate systems for determining the "master verse," and many Persian editions of Hafiz contain complicated mathematical tables for use in consulting the poet as an oracle. Aurungzeb, the Mogul Emperor, Nadir Shah and other rulers have let the Divan of Hafiz determine questions of peace and war. Some remarkably pat answers are of record, but not the times when the oracle has disappointed.

Hafiz was buried about two miles from Shiraz, in the gardens of Mosalla on the banks of the Ruknabad. The garden in which he lies is now known as the Hafiziya. A quatrain inscribed on his tomb gives the date* of his death as 1389. This date, however, is not necessarily accurate, for there is no proof that the quatrain is a contemporary one. Though its evidence is not unsupported, Muhammad Gulandam also giving 1389 as the year when Hafiz died, this date is not accepted as final by all scholars. Some books say that Hafiz died in 1391, and others 1388, 1390, 1394, etc.

A monument was built later over his grave, probably around 1452, by the grandson of Timur. Still later, about 1811, another of the poet's admirers, Vakil Kasim Khan

---

* According to Moslem custom, the date is hidden in the last line of the quatrain. It ends by ingeniously enjoining those who would know when Hafiz "sought a home in the dust of Mosalla to seek his date in the Dust of Mosalla." Dust of Mosalla in Persian is *Khak-i-Mosalla* (our word, khaki, coming from the Persian), and, letters in Persian having a numerical value as in Latin, the phrase equals 791 (After the Hegira, or 1389 A.D.).

Zand, placed a beautiful slab of alabaster over the tomb
on which is written:

> O *Thou*
> *Who endurest*
> *although*
> *all things pass away!*

To this are added *ghazal* 439 (in *Mim*) in its en-
tirety, from one stanza of which my *rubái* 56 is taken,
and the second stanza of *ghazal* 175 (in *Dal*), which I
give as *rubái* 98.*

The tomb of Hafiz has long been the place of pilgrim-
age that he foresaw. Persians go there to smoke, drink
and recite poetry. Many, indeed, have had their bodies
buried near that of the poet whom they name "the king of
the learned ones and the cream of the wise ones," "the
wonder of the time," "the interpreter of mysteries."
They call him *Lisan-ul-Ghaib*—The Tongue of the Hid-
den, "simple his speech and endless his meanings."

It is related that Hafiz was buried near a cypress tree
that he himself had planted for this purpose. If so, that
cypress no doubt has long since passed. But others have
grown in its place. Still is fulfilled the wish he once ex-
pressed to lie

> *Where some cypress will not tire*
> *His cooling shadow evermore to throw*
> *Upon the burning dust of my Desire.*

---

* My *rubái* 97 comes from the preceding stanza in this *ghazal*.

HAFIZ IN RUBAIYAT

*Transfuse the spirit of the original rather
than the mere expression.*—HORACE.

TRANSLATIONS of Hafiz do not lack. Readers of
them, unfortunately, do. The poet whose entire
Divan is known by heart by many Easterners even today
is, to all but a few Westerners, a shadowy name, or one
that has not that much substance.

The reason does not lie in the gulfs that separate us
from both Persia and the fourteenth century in which
Hafiz wrote. Not only do we find in Hafiz "those broad
and universal principles which, in every age and country,
are the same," (as Clarke has said), but some of his verses
apply even more to our age than to his. The stanzas on
prohibition at once come to mind, but the "modernity"
of others can hardly be less striking to a world enamoured
of the up-to-date, where the princes of public favour rise
and fall no less swiftly than did ever the favourites of
Oriental despots.

Shiraz, when the original of *rubái* 34 was written, did
not have the tabloid trumpet as an instrument for cham-

ber music. It did not know the breach of promise suit, the screeching mills of divorce that grind fast and exceeding coarse. The lines from which *rubái* 42 is drawn were not composed in a world with so many machines as ours for distracting man into dashing madly out of himself and over the face of the globe in the odd conviction that the faster and farther his body moves, the faster and farther goes his mind. The respect for mere mass, on which the Persian's comment is given in *rubái* 28, does not seem to have been so profound in his day as in ours, nor did the Kings of Kings referred to in *rubái* 58 have the means of humbler men today for emphasizing matter, whether in what passes for science or what passes for success in anything.

Hafiz does not date. The obscurity in which he has remained in our part of the world must be traced elsewhere. To my mind it can be traced, at least partly, to one phase of our habit of emphasizing matter. Forgetful of the words of Horace, we have come to think of translation as the reconstruction of a work done in one language by putting its expression, its most tangible element, as nearly as possible into the equivalent in another tongue.

Yet these tangible elements reveal the poet only as the corpse reveals the man. The delicate combination of them into a whole greater than its parts that gave them life is a secret known only to the Creator. To come nearly six hundred years later, when nothing but the bones remain, to make meticulous models of them in English plaster and to fit these together as closely as possible in the manner of the original, is to make only an artificial skeleton. Such skeletons have their place, but that place is not on the highways of life, nor yet even in the art galleries of museums.

The ideal of every translator, of course, is not merely to reproduce exactly the structure of the original, but to endow it with the same spark of life which its author gave it. The difficulty arises from the fact that this ideal can never be attained. If any of the three parts of the original—the form, the substance and the spirit—can be perfectly reproduced (which is rarely, if ever, possible), the subtle combination of the three can never be thus rendered.

The translator is driven to choosing which of these three elements he will emphasize the most: whether he will concentrate on reproducing the original poetic metre, or, casting metre to the winds, strive to give the exact wording in prose, or subordinate both metre and wording in an effort to make the spirit of the original live again. The metre and the wording form the easiest standards for comparing the original with the reproduction, and such stress has been placed on them that the nearer one attains to either, the more "faithful" his translation is called. Yet one (and particularly Hafiz) might well ask: "What doth it profit a poet to have his every word transcribed and to lose his own soul?"

I would not quarrel with the meaning translation has come to have. Translation in its usual sense (and it is the sense in which I employ the word throughout) has great value. I have emphasized its usual meaning in order to emphasize the more that I have not sought to give a translation. While all reproductions of a work in another tongue must be adaptations to a greater or less degree of its tangible elements, it is as well that we should call the latter translations and the former adaptations. Mine is an adaptation. It is a very free adaptation of the form and substance of the original. I have not sought to coax life into a skeleton or a mummy; I have sought to surround the immortal, the universal but the very elusive spirit of Hafiz with a living body.

It will help our acquaintance with Hafiz to consider in some detail the difficulties that those who would translate his expression, either in the sense of metre or of substance, or those who would transfuse his spirit, must face in the desire that prompts them all: to make him known and loved by readers of English.

It is not surprising that some should seek to gain this end by stressing above all the metre of the *ghazals* of Hafiz, for their music is one of the things for which he is loved by the Persians. But any poem is peculiarly the property of the language in which it is written. If words may be found in another language that have the same subtlety of meaning, or meanings, they will not have the same phonetic qualities and give the same subtle melody. This is true even of languages as closely allied to ours as French and German. It is far more true of Persian, in general, and even more of the *ghazals* of Hafiz.

To explain the rhythmical structure of the *ghazal* is to explain at once why the Divan can not be reproduced in English. At first glance it would not appear so difficult, for the *ghazal* may have from five to fifteen couplets and any Persian or Arabic metre, except that of the *rubái*, may be used. The first obstacle comes in the rhyming.

Not only do the lines of the first couplet rhyme, but the same rhyme must be used in the second verse of all the other couplets.* Moreover, the rhyming word throughout the *ghazal* must end in the same letter.

Persian is so rich in rhymes as to make this possible, not as a *tour de force* in one *ghazal*, but as the rule in hundreds of them. Hafiz not only has *ghazals* ending in each letter of the Persian alphabet, but he has a great many for nearly every letter. He has, for one instance, 166 *ghazals* rhyming throughout in words ending in the letter *Dal* (D) alone. The Divan, indeed, is arranged in all Persian texts with the *ghazals* grouped in alphabetical order, according to the last letter of the rhyming words in each of them.†

Even if it were possible to reproduce the Divan in English there would be no point in paying attention to its alphabetical arrangement, except for scholarly purposes, for the poems of Hafiz were not collected or arranged in any order by the poet himself. There are, for that matter, a number of Persian texts of the Divan of Hafiz, containing varying numbers of *ghazals* and with the poems, though always classified alphabetically, arranged in different numerical order under each letter.

* In the last couplet of the *ghazal*, the author nearly always addresses himself, so that the poem itself contains, in a way, the signature of the writer. This practice will explain the use of the name Hafiz in a number of my *rubáiyát*.
† In my references to certain couplets, I have given not only their serial number, as listed in Jarrett's text (*Divan-i Hafiz*. Calcutta: Urdu Guide Press, 1881), but also the name of the letter in which the rhyme ends, to aid in identifying them in other texts. Thus, the reference to *ghazal* 439 (in *Mim*) refers to *ghazal* 439 in Jarrett (or in Clarke's English prose translation of Jarrett) and to a *ghazal* that is listed under the letter "M" in all Persian texts containing it.

Moreover, as Jarrett points out, they vary in their readings of nearly every *ghazal*.*

The next difficulty has been touched upon in the foreword: Each couplet in the *ghazal* must convey a complete thought. The stanzas are strung like pearls on a necklace, the value of which, the Persians say, lies in the value of each pearl, not in the thread. Hafiz often paid so little attention to the thread on which he strung his pearls that, as has been noted, the incoherency of his *ghazals* drew criticism from Shah Shuja. Here, in merely four successive stanzas in *ghazal* 6 (in *Alif*), is a mild sample of what the Shah alluded to:

> The peace of the world is suspended from two hooks: goodwill and moderation.
> Fate has not received us. If we do not please you, change the orders of destiny.
> Wine, which is slandered, is worth more to us than the kiss of a virgin.
> Calm your irritation, my friend, for your mistress could make you melt like a candle.

This incoherence does not seem to have jarred on the ears of Persians other than this envious Shah, but it does tend to make Hafiz difficult reading for Westerners who are accustomed to more unity in a poem.†

* Jarrett, in his Persian text, follows that of Sudi as the most authentic, explaining, however, that even the Turk probably drew his from a manuscript of the fifteenth or sixteenth century, that is to say, dating no closer than three or four generations to the time when Hafiz died. With regard to some *ghazals* of doubtful origin Jarrett says:
   "If a punctilious criticism might hesitate to affirm their undoubted genuineness, it may nevertheless be forgiven to the fond idolatry of the East, if it chant the worship of its idol in numbers which seem to breathe his own inspiration."

† It should not be concluded that Hafiz is always incoherent, nor that there is not a beauty, in the long run and when the ear is trained to

The short of it is that the *ghazal* insists on an extremely difficult rhyme but allows the greatest licence with regard to matter, while our poetical practice reverses this, allowing much more liberty in rhyme and demanding far more unity in matter.

Despite the difficulties of the task, efforts have been made not only to reproduce the *ghazal* in English (usually as an ode), but John Payne has even translated the whole Divan of Hafiz in English verse in an attempt to follow as closely as possible the rhyme scheme of each *ghazal* in it as well as its matter. Walter Leaf aimed at the same precise metrical duplication but confined himself to a few *ghazals*. He frankly admitted that the music of Hafiz "defies the translator," but he has, however, given the best idea in English of both the music of the *ghazals* and their metre, or rather, their various metres. Some of his renditions are very ingenious, especially in view of all the handicaps his goal placed upon him. Yet, because of these handicaps, this method to my mind is generally fair neither to Hafiz nor to his translator.

The restrictions it involves give birth too often to something that is neither fish nor fowl. It is excellent Persian poetry forced into a mould never meant for it, so that it appears like an Aphrodite done with a corset. The reader, told that the translator has closely followed the

it, in the basic method of mingling themes closely together (a point that is dealt with later). Moreover, sometimes the incoherence of Hafiz is more apparent than real and the juxtaposition of two ideas, which seem to be distinct, serves to bring out an unsuspected relation between them, not the less powerfully for its subtlety. But since unity is required in the stanza rather than in the *ghazal*, one often can not be certain whether Hafiz intends a verse to be taken in its immediate context or not.

original Persian and ignoring all that makes such translation impossible, may conclude: If this is Hafiz, then he is vastly over-rated.

To avoid the pitfalls of this method, others, while keeping the *ghazal* intact, have adapted its metrical form and its matter much more freely in putting it in English, and they have confined themselves to translating only a few of the poems of the Divan, generally those that in one way or another lend themselves more readily to some English form. With some *ghazals*, especially those that are not incoherent, a fairly "close" and yet pleasing verse rendition may be and has been obtained. Gertrude Lowthian Bell's translation of selected *ghazals* is an excellent example of what can be done by this method.

But, by keeping the emphasis on the *ghazal* as a unit, when in the Persian the stress is on the individual stanza, this method tends to limit the presentation of Hafiz to the poems in which the thread connecting the pearls is more substantial than the rhyme, the only thread with which the original really needs to bother. It forces one to forego many a striking stanza because the *ghazal* containing it is so incoherent as to appear a jumble in English verse, or because the rest of the *ghazal* is not up to the same standard and might bury rather than bring out the thought.

While those who aim at a more or less close metrical translation of the *ghazal* strive also to express its substance, yet when one wants to know as nearly as possible what the poet wrote in so many words, he does not turn to verse renditions. He turns to those who have placed on themselves no metrical restrictions whatever and have adapted in the most radical manner the form Hafiz used, by putting his poetry into prose.

H. Wilberforce Clarke carried this method to its extreme. He set for himself the objective, not so much of expressing the thought of Hafiz as clearly as possible in English prose, but of translating the poems as literally as possible, not only word for word, but even to the arrangement of the words in each line. He meticulously carried this method through the whole Divan. There is distinct need for such scholarly works, and they have been of great help to me. Clarke's translation shows, however, how such endeavour may defeat its end of making Hafiz known. It results in English that, when it is not obscure or even meaningless, is frequently awkward.

Some examples that are by no means extreme will show his method. The lines from which I drew *rubái* 98 he translates as follows:

(O Saki of Alast) when, by the head of our tomb thou passest, ask for grace (for me),
For, the pilgrimage-place of the profligates (perfect lovers, comprehenders of the stages of love) of the world (the tomb of Hafiz)—shall be.*

Again, what I give as *rubái* 17, he renders:

The heart is the chamber (comprehender) of love of . . . His;
The eye is the mirror-holder (displayer) of the form of . . . His.

---

* *Alast* means *Eternity*. Clarke not only adds in parentheses words understood in the Persian text, as "(for me)", but, as has been noted, he also adds parenthetically the mystic interpretations given to some words such as "profligates (perfect lovers, etc.)".

83

> I, who incline not to the two worlds (this and the next),
> My neck is beneath the burden of favour of . . . His.*

As an example of his more straightforward prose, here is his translation of the couplet I give as *rubái* 36:

> Strike the bargain; purchase this shattered heart,
> That, despite its shattered state, is worth many an unshattered.

The French have developed the art of translating poetry into prose to a far higher degree than the English-speaking have. They employ a rhythmic prose that is at once clear and graceful. Charles Devillers, in the French *Ex Oriente Lux* edition of Hafiz, has been particularly successful, but he gives only a selection of *ghazals* and has dropped many couplets in them in order, no doubt, to diminish their incoherence. As an example of his method, here is his rendition of the lines that form the second of the citations just made from Clarke:

> Le coeur est l'écran derrière lequel se cache son Amour, son
> œil est le miroir qui réfléchit sa face,
> Moi qui ne courberais le front ni devant ce monde ni devant
> l'autre, j'incline très bas ma tête sous le joug de sa miséricorde.

Valuable as prose translations are, and however skillful they may be, prose is not poetry. One need only read the opening *rubái* of FitzGerald's Omar Khayyám, as given by Carpentier in "poetic" French prose, to see how much they lose:

---

* There is no way of determining in the Persian whether the pronoun here translated as "His" is really in the masculine and not the feminine, a fact that adds greatly to the ambiguity of Hafiz. Clarke almost always put such a pronoun in the masculine and gives a mystical version. Others put it in the feminine, so that it refers to human love.

Éveille-Toi! Car, à l'Est, là-bas, derrière la colline,
Le Soleil a chassé la Nuit et sa Théorie d'Etoiles;
* Et, en s'élançant dans les champs célestes,*
A frappé la Tour du Sultan d'un rayon de Lumière.

As some translations of Hafiz have concerned themselves with giving us as closely as possible his metrical expression, and as others have insisted in like manner on the literal expression of his thought, I have in my adaptation aimed above all at giving his spirit. Each of these methods sacrifices something, but by consulting all three versions one may perhaps gain a more complete idea of the poet in the original Persian.

My approach to the Divan of Hafiz may thus be analyzed: What is there in this verse (which, when literally translated into English, seems lifeless) that has made it live so long for those who read it in its original medium? The answer is that Hafiz made it live by concentrating on giving his thought the most beautiful, melodious—in a word, the most effective expression he could in Persian. He who would make that thought live in English now must subordinate everything in like manner to giving it effective expression.

The next question then is: What is the most effective verse form (for manifestly the poet must be rendered in verse, not prose) for its expression in English? The *ghazal*, we have seen, presents the problem an artist would have to face if he desired to paint effectively the foliage of a maple tree and had no green or means of making green. If he painted the leaves blue, he would be giving them his closest substitute for green, but the effect would be merely odd. Red is much farther removed from green than blue, but if the artist's object were to make men recognize and admire a living and beautiful maple tree, would he not be better advised to forget the springtime and give the tree the colours of autumn?

In seeking the most natural and effective colour on the English palette of verse to substitute for the Persian, it soon becomes evident that the beauty of Hafiz we seek to recapture lies for us in the individual stanza, rather than in the *ghazal*. The stanza is even more the unit for us than for the Persian, for by our inability to render effectively the rhyme of all the stanzas in the *ghazal*, we lose the one important thread that makes the binding together of these units charming in the original.

The problem thus narrows down to what is the best medium for expressing, in English verse, the complete thought in the stanza of Hafiz. His stanza is the couplet, but his couplets frequently vary in the number of feet in them and are often either so long as to be unwieldy in that form in English, or there is too much meaning packed in them to be brought out clearly in one of our couplets. Hafiz, moreover, uses his couplet to express a passionate or elevated sentiment, a witty thought, an epigram. Our most effective means of expressing such stanzas is not by our couplets, but by our *rubáiyát** or quatrains.

The *rubái*, as used by the Arabs, Persians and Turks, is a tetrastich in which the first three lines introduce the

* I say our *rubáiyát* because the *rubái* metre that FitzGerald made the standard for us, is not exactly the same as in Arabic or Persian, the line-units of which are most closely represented in English by the Alexandrine. FitzGerald, and Bicknell as well, found that this line of twelve syllables or six iambic feet was too heavy in English and reduced it to five feet.

thought, and the fourth may be, to give the Persian designations:

buland	. . .	elevated
latif	. . . .	witty, striking
tiz	. . . .	epigrammatical

The *rubái* is so plainly adapted to the stanza units of Hafiz that one may ask why he did not use this form. The answer is that he very evidently found a more effective form in the Persian *ghazal,* for his *ghazals* are far more famed in the East than the *rubáiyát* he did write, or the *rubáiyát* that any other Persian ever wrote. The question for us, however, is not what is the most effective medium for the Hafizian stanza in Persian, but what is in English, and the answer for us is the *rubái.*

Having settled on the *rubái* as the best medium, we come to the words Hafiz used to convey his thought. While his thought is limited neither by time nor place, it is clear that the means of expressing it which would be effective in the Persia in which he lived (and which has not changed so much as our world in the six centuries since then), might not always be so effective here and now. The civilization he knew differed from ours not only in time but in kind. There are the chasms between the Orient and the Occident, and between Islam and Christendom, to be bridged. They would not be so difficult to bridge, save for our colossal ignorance of all things Eastern and Islamic, an ignorance which is the harder to clear away since, even to reach it, one must first remove the tough fabric of prejudice with which the centuries have disguised it.

Because of these gulfs many of the allusions of Hafiz that, to the Persians for whom he wrote, add to his savour, mean to us little or quite nothing. The words of FitzGerald here take a meaning that he perhaps did not intend:

> What have we to do
> With Kaikobád the Great, or Kaikhosrú?

Some zealous translators have sought to solve this problem by devoting four-fifths of a page to footnotes explaining two lines of Hafiz. This scholarly work is to be praised, but not as poetry. Footnotes and poetry are peculiarly incompatible.

As the *ghazals* of Hafiz needed no footnotes or glossary for his contemporaries, I have sought to make my *rubáiyát* equally self-explanatory. I have tried first to understand for myself the significance of the names, allusions and figures of speech Hafiz uses. If his imagery served the specific and the general purpose (the best poetic expression of the thought) most effectively or as effectively in English, I have retained it. If it did not, I have sacrificed it for whatever might attain better for twentieth-century readers of English the central aim of the Persian of the fourteenth century.

This work of assimilation is comparable, as someone has said, to the scaffolding used in constructing a building. The structure could not go up without it, but to leave it standing when the work is done does not bring out the beauty of the building.

One example will help show the method used. The original of *rubái* 60 reads literally:

The Enka is not the prey of any man; draw in the nets,
For here nothing but wind is caught in the snare.

If one uses the word *Enka* he must add a note explaining that it is an Arabic name for a mythological creature, the word meaning one "whose name is known but whose body is lacking," and possibly referring to the phœnix, the bird of immortality. I have preferred to incorporate this explanation in the *rubái* itself to bring home the meaning of the picture.

When I have departed freely from the original in applying this method I have sought, however, to use images that are the common heritage both of the East and the West*, and to keep within the spirit of the Divan as a whole. Thus, a poet may use a variety of images, at one time or another, to express much the same thing. Where I have found one of these synonymous images in the Divan better adapted to English than the one in the stanza being rendered, I have used it, instead.

The choice of words and images, moreover, forms but a part of something greater, which may be called style. It has seemed to me that the general manner by which Hafiz contrives to express an idea effectively in his own medium was the thing to stress most in giving that basic thought in English. Among the things that characterize

---

* The fact that Mohammed in the Koran tells of Adam, Noah, Abraham, and other figures of the Old Testament, as well as of Jesus Christ, all of whom he recognizes as prophets, contributes to the common heritage of Islam and Christendom. The allusion by Hafiz to Noah, from which *rubái* 13 is drawn, is, indeed, even more effective for Christians than for Moslems. The Prophet, in his version of Noah, seems to have suppressed (perhaps because of his hatred for wine) that part of the Biblical story which relates that after leaving the Ark "Noah began to be an husbandman, and he planted a vineyard: And he drank of the wine, and was drunken."

his style, and that I have sought to preserve, are lightness of touch, irony, restraint, antithesis, subtlety, saying one thing that on the surface is beautiful in itself but reveals new beauties and new meanings the more one reads it, and introducing a thought in such a way that its climax has the doubled force of the unexpected and the logical.

Finally, in following the principle of trying to give Hafiz as effectively as I could, I have occasionally contracted into one *rubái* ideas expressed in a whole *ghazal* or in several couplets, whether contiguous or separated. In like manner I have at other times expanded a single couplet into more than one *rubái,* or combined both methods. There is no language that I know in which some things can not be said more concisely than in English, and in which other ideas can be stated with its brevity. One must use one's judgment in contracting here and expanding there, as the occasion demands. Most of the *rubáiyát,* however, are drawn from a single stanza in some *ghazal.**

After deciding on the most effective method for presenting Hafiz there remains the question: What is the meaning contained in the Hafizian stanza? What is its central thought that we have chosen our instruments to express? The problem it presents is a very difficult one.

One need only start on the logical road from the simple to the complex to divine how hard it is to know just

* To the exceptions noted I would add that two *rubáiyát,* 23 and 67, are drawn from *rubáiyát* written by Hafiz, while another, *rubái* 71, is from one of the brief isolated poems classed as "fragments." Several critics say that this latter refers to the death of the son of Hafiz, but as the text is vague as to the identity of the lost one, I have preferred to make its application equally general.

what Hafiz meant. Whatever Frenchman first said, "*La parole a été donnée à l'homme pour déguiser sa pensée*," phrased enduringly the difficulties that everyone has encountered in making himself understood by contemporaries who share his mother tongue—the easiest form of communication.

Hafiz is far removed from us in language, time, place and civilization, and the several texts of his Divan often conflict. To all the opportunites for misunderstanding that each of these provides, the Persian adds some all his own. We can not depend on his context, as with other authors, to throw light on his specific meaning. There is the more need for such light, since, as one critic has said, Hafiz seems to have had for his device: "More sense than words." FitzGerald, struck by this quality of the poet, wrote to Cowell that Hafiz's "sonnets are sometimes as close packt as Shakespeare's, which they resemble in more ways than one."

Known and loved for his subtlety, the oracle of Shiraz is frequently more than Delphically cryptic even for the most learned Persians. It seems probable that this was at least partly due to his need for protecting his person. Whatever the cause, one must always keep in mind, in reading Hafiz, that all is not necessarily what it seems on the surface. One must be on the alert for a hidden meaning. There are pretty pebbles on the shore, but, as Saie says, one must dive for the pearls.

It is small wonder, then, that opposed schools of philosophy claim Hafiz as their champion, that learned scholars give as many as ten possible interpretations of a single phrase of his and that foreign renditions of the same

91

verse vary sharply, and are often as opposed as black and white.

All that anyone can do is to follow in Hafiz the counsel that Kamal of Khujand* gave to his own readers:

> When the Divan of Kamal comes to your hand,
> Copy as much of his verse as you will.
> But if you wish to understand aright
> His rare expressions, words and thoughts,
> Do not fly, like the pen, over each word,
> But dive, like the ink, into each letter.

Even so, no one can pretend to certainty. Has not Hafiz himself written:

> Do not waste your wit or your sagacity on the verses of Hafiz:
> His pen has secrets that you do not know.

In putting these lines into *rubái 79*, it struck me that the best proof of the truth they contained lay in the fact that no author can himself know what his words will mean to all his contemporaries, to say nothing of foreigners who read them centuries later. The haughty barons who wrote *Magna Charta* did not dream that hundreds of years later it would be interpreted as the charter of freedom for commoners whom they despised even more than they did John Lackland. It seemed to me that the variety of conflicting interpretations given both in Persia and elsewhere to any one passage of Hafiz threw some light on the hidden sense of this particular couplet, and I put this in the last line of my *rubái*.

* Kamal was a contemporary whom Professor Browne says won the admiration of Hafiz.

As the wise Abu Suoud said, everyone must judge for himself the meaning to be ascribed to the poems of Hafiz. I have formed my own conception of Hafiz, as must everyone of any author, and I have sought merely to give effectively to others what Hafiz gave to me. To get his meaning I have compared various translations in English and French and have consulted the original text with the help of a Persian friend, Mehmed Ali Haji Baba.* Withal, I have used my own judgment. The meanings Hafiz gave to me differ frequently and sometimes radically from those he has given to others, just as these others differ among themselves. It may very well be that I have not always got the thought Hafiz intended to give me. Hafiz himself made clear how little assurance it behooves anyone to have about his meaning, when he showed how basic must be our uncertainty about anything:

Since the Beloved has veiled his face, how is it that his lovers are describing his beauties?
They can only relate what they imagine is there.

My *rubáiyát*, I would emphasize, represent only a slight fraction of the stanzas in the Divan of Hafiz. In selecting them, however, I have sought to give the major themes in the Divan, and in arranging them I have aimed to give the effect they have for me in the complete collection. The frequent juxtaposition in the *ghazal* itself of these themes, together with the juxtaposition in the Divan of *ghazals* in which they are treated, now separately and

* I can not let this occasion pass without expressing my thanks to Mehmed Ali, who first made me acquainted with Hafiz while acting as my interpreter during a trip through Asia Minor in 1921, and who has been of invaluable assistance to me in this present work.

now together, has an effect, when one's ear is tuned to it, that can best be likened to counterpoint in a symphony.

We have the central, underlying theme, which is Hafiz's philosophy or attitude toward life and which runs through the *ghazal* and through the Divan. We have other themes, such as those that may be called love, wine, and the secret of existence. They are closely allied to each other and to the central motif, and yet in a certain sense they are individual.

From one theme, as in thought itself and as in Beethoven, another is born and from it another. They rise and fall and recur again in a somewhat different tone in the Divan as in a symphony. Sometimes they seem to die of themselves, sometimes they strive with one another for mastery, sometimes for a moment one seems to dominate and sometimes when one seems forgotten a bold note reminds us that it is still somewhere near.

A faraway piping lures one from the melancholy of a baffling secret of existence to love, and the violins, hearkening, soar into passion. Then, when the whole orchestra seems to be under the sway of the theme, this very concentration destroys its own objective. The different instruments assert themselves like the mind considering a thought from every angle. Love is pursued to its end in the same baffling maze, and, in the pursuit, the theme of wine gradually seduces or suddenly seizes the orchestra. Off it goes on another tack in its effort to reach some port, until, finding that the sea is without a shore, the 'cellos pick up the love motif again. Sadly and with less assurance, the orchestra re-examines it and is led back to the theme of wine. They mingle, dispute, and rise alternately to mastery while the swelling undertone of the bass viols comes out momentarily like wind heard in the trees when battles lull, and suddenly it carries the orchestra with a crash back to the ultimate secret. Thus the symphony goes on until the themes with all their variations are wrought into the central motif from which they developed and which they themselves have so developed in turn that they have become subordinate though still very living parts of the whole.

The process by which the spirit that I conceive to be Hafiz reveals itself more and more clearly in his Divan is much too delicate and subtle to be analyzed and described. It may be felt, however, by those for whom Beethoven does not simply produce beautiful sounds but harmonizes them into revealing the soul of man. Feeling this innate harmony in the Divan, I have tried to arrange some bars of the master in a score that might, in like manner, make his spirit felt in English.

A word remains to be said about the epilogue and the proem. The epilogue is my own, but the thought in it is not foreign to Hafiz—at least, not to my Hafiz. As for the proem, it should not be inferred that Saie wrote it with Hafiz in mind. Nor were his lines adapted by me for the purpose they here serve. Saie, who lived in Constantinople in the sixteenth century, composed the poem as an apology for the life of Sinan that he wrote from data given him by that great Turkish architect. An admirer of the many works of Sinan, I sought to learn more about him, and one day in the Bazaar in Stamboul I found this story that Saie told, partly in prose and partly in verse.

In putting it into English, it seemed to me that the apology, written in rhymed couplets in the original Turkish, lost much of its beauty and force when rendered in that form in our tongue. In experimenting, I happened on the *rubáiyát* adaptation. About this time I chanced to be reading a French prose translation of Hafiz. Struck by a verse, I had the idea of trying to bring out its meaning, too, in *rubái* form. Thus this version of Hafiz grew from the apology of Saie. And the more I worked with Hafiz, the more some of the words of the Turk seemed to apply to the Persian—and others to my adaptation of him.

THE DECORATIONS

The decorations in Persian script are by Hafiz Nejmeddin Effendi, professor of calligraphy at the Stamboul School of Calligraphy, Constantinople. He has done them in three styles of writing that were much in favour in Persia in the time of Hafiz.

The bars bordering the *rubáiyát* are alternately in *nasikh* and *sulus*, both of which originated in Bagdad in the era immortalized for the West by the *Arabian Nights. Nasikh* (which may be identified in the bars enclosing *rubáiyát* 10 to 15) was created by Ibn Mokla, who is as celebrated an old master in Islam, where calligraphy enjoys the esteem we accord to painting, as Raphael in Christendom. *Sulus* (enclosing *rubáiyát* 16 to 21) is attributed both to Kotba and to Ibrahim Segzi. Persian illuminated manuscripts of the time of Hafiz frequently use *nasikh* and *sulus* alternately.

The text of the inscriptions in both styles is the same throughout. The bar at the top reads: *Lisan-ul-Ghaïb : Khajeh Shams-ud-Din Mohammed Hafiz Shiraz-i : Rahmat-ul-Lahi Aaleyhi* [The Tongue of the Hidden : The Old Master Shams-ud-Din Mohammed Hafiz of Shiraz : May He Rest in Peace.] The Moslem *requiescat in pace* has been added in fulfillment of the wish expressed by Hafiz in the couplet appearing on his tomb and forming the text of the bottom bars in this book. From this couplet my *rubái* 98 was drawn.

The script on the cover is in *sulus,* with the name, *Hafiz,* written on the right and *Lisan-ul-Ghaïb* on the left.

The line on the title page, like that on the fly-leaf, is in the style called *nastalik,* created by one of the most renowned of the Persian masters, Mir Ali, a contemporary of Hafiz. The text is the same as that of the bars above the *rubáiyát.*

Printed in the United States
99538LV00005B/159/A